Should There Be Space Exploration?

A Persuasive Text

Written by

Susan Harvey's Fifth Grade Students

Acknowledgments

The authors would like to thank the following people:

The Tewksbury Education Foundation for funding our mini-grants for a trip to the Buehler Challenger and Space Center

Our fifth grade teachers, Mrs. Ruane, Mrs. DenBleyker, Ms. Leber, Mrs. Condron, and Mr. Steinman, for letting us leave class to work on this enrichment project with Mrs. Harvey

Our librarian, Mrs. Larson, for helping us locate resources

Our parents

Our editor, Susan Eddy, at Mondo Publishing

All photographs © 2006 by John Paul Endress unless otherwise noted.
Simulated space activities and student astronaut portraits photographed at the
Buehler Challenger and Science Center, Paramus, New Jersey, January 2006.
Cover, u.l., u.r., 7 b., 16, 18 b., 23, 24 b., 28 b: NASA. 8, 17, 19, 21, 26, 29 t., 30, 31 b., 47:
Buehler Challenger and Science Center. 4, 13, 37, 39, 40, 43, 44, 45, 46: Harvey/Larson.

Text copyright © 2007 by Mondo Publishing

For information contact:
Mondo Publishing
980 Avenue of the Americas
New York, NY 10018

Visit our website at www.mondopub.com

Printed in China
08 09 10 11 12   9 8 7 6 5 4 3 2
ISBN 1-59336-827-5

Design by Jean Cohn

Contents

QUESTION:
What does the sun want to be when it grows up?

Introduction

What Is Space?

Before you start reading our book, you will need to understand the term *space.* Space is non-ending. It is home to everything you've ever seen or heard of, or that exists without our even knowing. Some people call it the universe, others call it the cosmos, or even just atmosphere.

To write this book, we've taken the issue of space exploration and broken it into ten basic categories: satellites, the moon, Mars, robots, space money, Hubble Space Telescope, International Space Station, ocean exploration, Earth's needs, and even space pollution! We've tried to decide whether we need some of these things, or if some are absolutely absurd and unnecessary. Space is, and will be, a mystery for a very long time—maybe even forever. We wanted to see if it would be worth it to investigate and "crack the code." So, should there be space exploration? Pretty soon you'll find out what we think.

What Is Persuasive Text?

At our first meeting as authors, we were asked if we knew what on Earth (!) a persuasive text is. Everyone struggled—we were completely baffled by the question. We started guessing, and finally someone guessed right! Persuasive text is a type of writing that tries to persuade the reader to agree with the writer's point of view. In this book, since there are 11 writers, there are 11 points of view—some pro, some con. You'll even find that one writer changed her mind as she did her research. She went from con to pro.

The Sign

After every article, you'll see a little Earth that looks either

like this 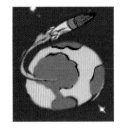 or like this.

The Earth with the rocket (left) means that the author is *for* space exploration (pro). The Earth with the flower (right) means that the author is *against* space exploration (con). In one article you will see both icons. That author changed her mind.

Never Fear, A Glossary Is Here!

You might have noticed some blue words like *pro* and *con.* That's because you can check in the glossary and find the meanings of those words. It is very easy and simple to read. The entries are short and complete. The glossary includes just about all the tough words in the entire book that you might not understand.

Mars: Needed for Our Future

"...I suggest we continue our efforts to explore Mars. One day that might be a future home to world citizens because of the problems we are creating here on Earth."

—JOHN PARKER

Rapidly, every day, Earth is growing more polluted and populated. We need to do something about those two major problems. The United States has begun space exploration, and I suggest we continue our efforts to explore Mars. One day that might be a future home to world citizens because of the problems we are creating here on Earth. NASA should begin their efforts by sending more rovers and at least one manned mission in the near future to work towards a Mars/humankind goal. In fact, President George Bush built that objective into the NASA budget in 2004. Other countries believe in the program and have formed partnerships in our space exploration efforts.

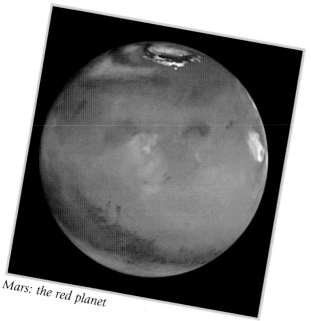

Mars: the red planet

The Viking I and II U.S. Landers (remote-control, life-size cars/robots) took the first steps exploring in 1975. Their task was to test for life on Mars. Some scientists think the tests in Vikings I and II's onboard labs proved that there was no life on Mars. Other scientists think it's still unclear, and that life may have once existed. These two scientific views are one of the

— 7 —

reasons we should continue exploring Mars.

Another one of the most important questions concerning Mars is whether or not there is water. People thought that there was water back in 1890, when an Italian astronomer thought he saw canals on Mars. That started the "alien" age, with stories about Martian invasions. If there was Martian life, which scientists believe is unlikely, it would have been very long ago. The exploration of Mars by Viking I proved the Italian astronomer's idea of water wrong. But there are still some scientific notions that underground reservoirs did exist which, if unleashed, could cover all of Mars with oceans 1,000 feet deep.

Because of our explorations, now and in the future, there may be space colonies on Mars to look forward to. An important task is first to send astronauts to Mars to see what it is like through human eyes. The cost will be very expensive—approximately $600 billion—and very risky. Many times this is the reason people don't want Mars exploration, but I think that in life you have to take some risks.

Living on Mars would be very hard for humans. The pressure of the atmosphere is so low that if you stepped out unprotected, your blood would boil. You would have to dress warmly—when the Viking I landed, the temperature averaged about–190° F (–123°c) at midday and at night about 45° F (7°c). Gravity is also different from what we are used to. It is about one-third of our gravity. People have used a bit of humor talking about what we might need on Mars. How about electronic eyes to resist the cold, artificial or fake lungs to turn carbon dioxide into oxygen, plastic skin to resist dangerous chemicals, and bat wings—not for flying, but to get solar energy?

Although normal life on Mars may seem impossible now, I think it will be possible in the future. Perhaps we should begin by setting microbes free on Mars. It may take a very long time, maybe even 5,000 years, but we may have a planet on which generations to come might live like they do here on Earth. NASA has planned a manned mission to Mars in 2025 and is considering building a permanent base. I think that these starting steps, as well as a belief in space exploration, are vital to human survival.

Space vs. Earth

"Space exploration seems foolish when we have so many more important things we should work with on Earth."

—CORTNEY COX

In June of 2000, President Bill Clinton said, "...more than 95 percent of the underwater world remains unknown and unseen. What remains to be explored could hold clues to the origins of life on Earth, links to our maritime history, to cures for disease." That statement, along with the fact that over 70 percent of our globe is covered with water, and that more than 97 percent of that water is oceans, is amazing. It is time for all people to respond to this unknown, unseen, and unacceptable situation. I recommend that we begin by canceling the United States space program.

In 2006 approximately $16.5 billion was budgeted for NASA space exploration, and only a fraction of that amount for Earth exploration. Not only does "exploring" space cost a lot of money, it also costs a lot of money to find spaceships when they get lost. In 1999 the Mars Polar Lander got lost, and more than $120 million was spent just to find it! In 2006 NASA asked for $374 million just to make the space shuttle safe to fly again. And that is not all.

Marcie McNutt of California's Monterey Bay Aquarium Bay Research Institute estimates that the government spends only one-tenth on ocean studies of what it pays for space exploration. What that means is for every ten dollars the government spends on space exploration, it spends only one dollar on ocean exploration. That doesn't seem fair, does it? When we explore the ocean, we often find something new and important, living and non-living, to improve our lives. These new things could be food, medicines, building materials, or new ways to uncover and repair damages caused by pollution.

Besides exploring our oceans, space exploration money could be spent on dealing with pollution on Earth. Scientists are very worried that when people pollute our planet, it affects the atmosphere. Because of global warming, the ice at the North Pole is slowly melting. The melting causes Arctic animals like polar bears to lose their homes and lives. Almost 1,500 species of animals have changed their ways because of climate change. Our polluted atmosphere may not allow their survival. Global warming may also hinder other living things—plants, and even the humans on our planet. That means you and me, and I want to fight that. But it takes money.

One interesting kind of pollution is debris that comes from rockets, shuttles, and robots. Space exploration is polluting space! Natural disasters are also natural polluters. Volcanoes with lava, gases, and lava bombs can shoot out and kill plants, animals, and people. Tsunamis and hurricanes can hurt Earth by causing massive destruction to living things and by creating unsafe and unsanitary conditions that require money to get cleaned up. Both cause destruction of our necessary natural resources. These natural polluters are just as important as the unnatural ones. But it takes money to respond to them.

Space exploration seems foolish when we have so many more important things we should work with on Earth. People have to realize that space exploration is an expensive fantasy that we need to stop paying so much attention to. I am against it, and I certainly am against any funds being used for such destruction.

Satellites: An Important Part of Space Exploration and Our Daily Lives

"Space exploration helps make...many things we enjoy possible." —CAROLINE OLESIAK

Think about not having a phone, a computer, or even a television. Wouldn't that be awful? Read on and find out why, without satellites and space exploration, we might not have the technology that allows us to have these important tools in our lives.

When you hear the words *space exploration*, I'll bet satellites never cross your mind. In fact, what are satellites? They are objects in orbit, rotating around another, larger body (such as another planet)—like our moon. The moon is our sixth largest satellite, and it is our only natural satellite.

There are approximately 8,000 man-made satellites orbiting Earth, plus over 16,000 pieces of junk. Some satellites have important jobs, although many of the objects left in space are "orbital trash." They are parts, such as lenses, hatch covers, rocket bodies, payloads that have exploded, and other objects released from certain spacecraft during their tasks. If you ever look up to see the stars shortly after dusk or right before dawn, you may notice only one or two stars. But maybe they are not stars. They may be Earth-orbiting satellites. If you have binoculars or a telescope, you might be able to see hundreds of them.

Satellites are immense, complex machines. Many do thousands of tasks every day, depending on the orbit they are in. They send us signals that provide hundreds of television channels across the globe. That doesn't sound like a big job, but have you ever thought about the jobs the televisions do? An example is the Weather Channel. Every day pictures are sent from satellites to many weather stations. The meteorologists can then tell us what the weather is going to be.

Not only are there communication and weather satellites, but there are also others that help the military, that help map our world and our skies, and that help us try to figure out what our universe might contain. I'm sure that you have heard of the Global Positioning System (GPS) because many cars and boats now have it. The GPS satellites are used for navigation almost anywhere on Earth. Also, pictures taken from space let mapmakers know about the physical aspects of our planet.

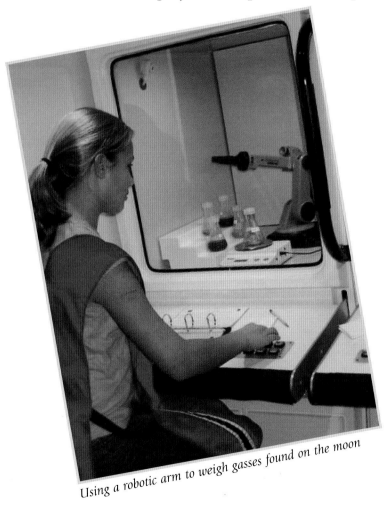

Using a robotic arm to weigh gasses found on the moon

Man-made satellites have two main parts: a payload and a bus. The payload is all the cameras and material needed to do the jobs the satellite was sent to do. A bus holds all the instruments in the payload together and keeps it all going.

Satellites are able to stay in space because they are going very fast, and gravity is pulling them down and stabilizing them in orbit. (That is, unless a drag happens, and the air slows them down.) All of this happens without an engine. The sun is their engine! How is that? Most satellites have solar panels, and the panels contain solar cells. Those cells change sunlight into electricity. Some people even think that some day, satellites can collect solar power to be used on Earth. Satellites take pictures of Earth and also travel to other planets in our solar system to take pictures. Space stations like the International Space Station could not exist without the use of many satellites.

I have chosen to tell you why I think space exploration is important. People could definitely live without the television, phone, and computer, but I don't know anyone who would even consider it in today's world. Space exploration helps make these and many more things we enjoy possible.

The Hubble Telescope: Is It Worth the Money?

"I…wonder if the expensive telescope has taken pictures of the pollution NASA is creating in space, and whether it will become part of that pollution." —ALICE ROLL

I wonder if the very expensive Hubble Space Telescope has taken pictures of the pollution we have created on Earth, and I wonder if it is worth the money that could have been spent cleaning up that pollution. I also wonder if the expensive telescope has taken pictures of the pollution NASA is creating in space, and whether it will become part of that pollution.

The Hubble Space Telescope was sent into space by NASA on the back of a space shuttle in 1990. It orbits 375 miles (604 k) from Earth and now takes photographs that amaze us. Some are pictures of huge dust storms on Mars that have covered more than half the planet. A dust storm is when dust that usually lies on the ground is swept up into the air and creates a storm. Hubble has also taken pictures of stars. It takes them when the stars are born, while they are alive, and at their death. The death of a star is known as a nebula. A nebula looks like a regular explosion except about 100 times bigger. Many of the photographs have taught us important facts about Earth and are needed by NASA for their exploration. Recently Hubble discovered new rings and moons around Uranus. But—the Hubble cost $1,500,000 to build and get into orbit. Then every year it costs about $240 million more to take care of it! That is a large amount not spent on the needs of Earth and its people.

Although the Hubble is still working, NASA may replace it with a new telescope. The James Webb Space Telescope will cost $825,000,000 to send into space. That is $823,500,000 more than the Hubble! This amount does not include the cost to send people into space to service it— to make sure everything is working properly and to install new instruments. Yes, the James Webb will be a better telescope, but it will be further away and will, therefore, cost more to service. Once again, what about our needs on Earth?

Servicing the Hubble Space Telescope

NASA has said that they may shut down the Hubble naturally by not servicing it, or they may send a repair mission to service it. Without repairs, they expect it to take about six years to shut down. During that time NASA will be focusing on the James Webb. Is it possible that this neglect might lead to space pollution? Could part of the Hubble chip or break off and join the other litter that is slowly filling up space?

The part of space that is nearest to Earth is becoming increasingly populated by man-made junk, some put there by astronauts while they are on their jobs. Space is also littered with space junk, including old satellites, burned-out rockets, and rockets that have exploded. Every single time someone sends spacecraft into space, they leave their mark with some sort of litter. And that space debris is dangerous! Because it travels about eight miles per second, a paint chip that is the size of your pinky fingernail could kill an astronaut by piercing his or her spacesuit. More than 80 shuttles have had to have their windshields replaced because of space debris. I wonder how much that replacement costs! A medium-sized piece of space debris could do enough damage to blow up an entire spacecraft. That would make even more space debris. What if some of that debris came down to Earth?

The earth is polluted, and we have now begun to pollute space, too. The Hubble may be replaced by a more expensive telescope. Six years of Hubble explorations and funding are being thrown away. How can we justify spending money on these and not spending it on Earth's needs? I can't.

Space Exploration With Humans or Robots?

"With today's knowledge, we can program robots do even greater things." —CARA SOLINA

Humans exploring space—a common, everyday thought. But imagine if humans didn't have to explore space, and let robots do the work. It would save us so much—and not just money. With robots exploring space, you would turn around your every doubt about space exploration.

Robots would help us because they are capable of doing the completely amazing. They've already done things humans will never have any hope of doing. They have taken breathtaking pictures of Mars's rust and dried lake beds, Jupiter's 63 moons, and the sun's lava-hot surface. Now we must take advantage of their amazing capabilities and kick it up a notch. With today's knowledge, we can program robots to do even greater things.

Robots can do many things for space organizations like NASA, and they can save the United States a lot of time and money. Robots save money because they do not need what we humans call necessities, like food, water, and spacesuits. Some robots don't even need a spaceship. Time is also another good thing about robots. Unlike humans, robots don't need to sleep or take breaks. I'm not saying that astronauts are lazy, but instead of snoring

The FIDO rover is a robot that simulates driving conditions on Mars

like humans, robots could be doing more actual work.

Robots could also help prevent tragedies like the Columbia spacecraft incident. Instead of those seven people dying, a few robots could've been lost. As a member of the British government said, "If a robot goes missing, it is an expensive shame, but if a pod full of people were to crash onto the surface of Mars it would be a catastrophe." Also, people on spaceships can suffer serious damage from space flight. Weightlessness causes bones to weaken and can hurt the immune system. People can also lose bone mass and red blood cells from the lack of gravity. These things could be harmful to an astronaut's body.

It is not impossible for robots to explore space. If people were replaced by robots, many of our space-travel issues, such as money, the astronauts' safety, and other things, would be solved. This could make exploring space completely worth the effort. We should definitely have space exploration, but only if more robots are involved. With robots, the United States and other countries could take giant leaps toward success.

Animals in Space?
It Is Certainly Not Their Choice!

"I am almost certain that if animals could talk, they would say "no" to this risk." —DANA JENNINGS

Back in the 1950s, scientists in Russia and the United States were preparing to send humans into space. Before astronauts could travel on spaceships, research on living creatures was needed. Stress and weightlessness were major concerns. Rather than take any chances with humans, scientists tested animals to see what might happen. What does this have to do with my feelings about our space program today? Astronauts have a say in their role in exploring space. Do animals? I am almost certain that if animals could talk, they would say "no" to this risk.

The following is the first sad story about an animal is space, Dog Laika. I came to like Dog Laika when I had to do a research project about him for class. That assignment made me realize that I am against space exploration because of the cruelty to animals.

Dog Laika was a Russian dog that was sent into space on Sputnik II, a Russian spaceship. The ship had a capsule that was specially designed to keep her body temperature and heart rate normal. It also had a machine that could feed her. Monitors were hooked up, but

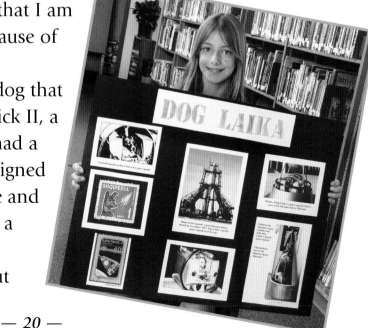

Buehler & Challenger
Space & Science Center 2006

Dog Laika died three minutes after takeoff. We were told that she orbited Earth seven times before she died. This was certainly not the truth! And the really sad part is that minutes after takeoff, the Russian program told the world that this trip was planned to be one-way. The spaceship was not even designed to get the dog back alive!

Another sad story happened about one year later. The United States decided it was time to study space travel using monkeys. The first monkey was a squirrel monkey that they named Gordo. He was placed on the Jupiter AM-13 booster rocket. It looked like Gordo was going to come back alive. But the capsule landed in the ocean, sank, and Gordo died. This did not stop our space program from using monkeys, and there were many animals that returned home alive. But who knows what it was like for them in space?

Animals, including fish and baby mammals, are still taken into space, usually to see how they react to microgravity. Even though we have had some successful explorations, I feel that the space program is very expensive, unnecessary to the most important things needed on Earth, risky to astronauts' lives, and cruel to animals. Remember, an animal does not have the choice that a human being has. Why should we make animals suffer for space exploration? We should not.

Step One: Robots
Step Two: Robots and Humans

"I believe in space exploration and see it as a necessity for humankind."
—HARRISON BERGMAN

Much of the technology that affects our lives is developed through our space program. That technology makes us look past Earth and into the unknown universe where we might begin to learn about our future. I believe in space exploration and see it as a necessity for humankind. But I have two steps that NASA should follow. The first involves only robots, and the second involves a partnership between robots and people.

My two steps for NASA to follow are based on money and safety. Right now it's estimated that a manned mission to Mars would cost about $50–100 billion. But all of the rover robot missions to Mars so far have only cost $4.2 billion! Robert Park, a physics professor at the University of Maryland, says "The usual factor that's used to do anything in space is that it costs at least 10 times as much to do it with a human as it does to do the same thing robotically. I think it's closer to 100."

People believe that humans' quick thinking is an asset in space exploration because of two well-known situations, Apollo 13 and Skylab. But in a recent simulation, space experts experienced a situation where they could control a robot's movements just as they would their own bodies. There is only one problem with this. If the distance between the NASA controller and the robot becomes more than a light second (186,000 miles or 300,000 km), there begins to be lag time in the signals. But they can avoid

Mars exploration rover deploying robotic arm for rock study

this by simply preprogramming any long-distance robots. More importantly, if worse comes to worst and there are no humans to "save the day," lives aren't lost—only metal is.

Robots have some physical capabilities that far exceed those of humans, allowing them to travel easily on land that might be destructive to us. And people have yet to travel on a successful mission that passes the moon, while robots are exploring Jupiter! Based on examples like these, children think of robots as superstrong machines, but this isn't true—at least not on Earth. A robot's strength on Earth is equal to that of a person's, but in microgravity (weightlessness experienced in the orbit of a planet) robots are much stronger than people (although they are not always as accurate).

When we are able to lower costs and risks to human life, we should begin Step Two: a partnership of robots and humans. The partnership will allow space missions and long-term objectives to progress faster. Humans might conduct tests while robots steer the shuttle. Maybe we'll even have a space station on Mars where humans live and robots travel back and forth to Earth for supplies. What we think of as science fiction might some day be accomplished if humans and robots work together.

The International Space Station

"ISS allows people from the United States and other countries to work together to learn about space and to conduct experiments we cannot do here on Earth." —EMILY PASSERA

Since I was very little, I've dreamed about space exploration. Lots of people "wish upon a star" and think about what is up there. Now we have started having our dreams and questions answered by the International Space Station!

The International Space Station (ISS), home to several astronauts and cosmonauts (Russian astronauts), is orbiting 240 miles (386 km) above Earth at this very time. The ISS allows people from the United States and other countries to work together to learn about space and to conduct experiments we cannot do here on Earth. We share the cost and the work with other countries to learn new things in medicine, science, and other areas that will help everyone on Earth. People are willing to help despite their differences. They demonstrate that space has no owner by working together. Sixteen countries are involved with the ISS. They include the United States, Russia, Japan, Italy, France, the Netherlands, Canada, Brazil, the United Kingdom, Belgium,

International Space Station

Denmark, Norway, Spain, Germany, Sweden, and Switzerland. Each of the countries is making parts for the ISS. It will not be finished until 2010, but it is already showing lots of possibilities for the future.

The ISS is going into space piece by piece. Manned and unmanned shuttles are putting the pieces in compartments and blasting them into orbit. It is hard work! People must train for the unexpected by doing simulated missions. A lot of work goes into that, but I think it is worth it.

During an average day on the ISS, astronauts wake up at 6:00 A.M. and eat three meals a day that they ordered five months before their flight. Astronauts perform maintenance and do experiments, like studying bees living in less gravity and recording the earth's position. The astronauts also have to exercise and sleep. As regular humans, they sometimes just relax, watch DVD's, and play silly games or call home. In space they can be weightless and not cramped in a shuttle or limited because their spacesuits have only so much air if they want to go outside. It sounds like fun to be an astronaut. I think the only boring part is the trip up to the ISS. It takes only eight minutes to get into space, but two days to get to the ISS!

On April 4, 2001, Daniel S. Goldin of NASA, said "NASA's high priority goals are: 1) to have permanent human presence in space, 2) have international partnerships and 3) world-class searches in space." Who knows what good things could happen with so many countries working together? The International Space Station orbits over Earth's atmosphere with astronauts watching, experimenting, and even helping us on Earth. I want my dreams to come true. I want people to continue to go into space, and I want to learn new and wonderful things about space exploration.

How to Help Earth and Not Space

"Instead of space exploration, let's fund programs that provide disaster relief, prevent animal cruelty, and protect our environment." —ARNAV JINDIA

Billions of dollars are spent on space exploration every year. NASA's current five-year budget is $86 billion. The budget for 2006 alone is $16.5 billion. The International Space Station (ISS) may end up costing $100 billion! Some figure it has already cost about $75 billion. That is a lot of money for finding the unknown when we already know of needs on our Earth. Why not cut the expense and use it for some basic needs on our own planet? It is our duty to help today's people. So instead of space exploration, let's fund programs that provide disaster relief, prevent animal cruelty, and protect our environment. The following are examples of the many good programs we could support.

The American Red Cross is an organization that relies on donations and volunteers. Their job is to help people during disasters and to respond to major emergencies, such as Hurricane Katrina. They help people around the world with many services, such as medical needs, health, and safety problems. The Red Cross has programs that assist people so they can lead safer and healthier lives. Training programs for people to learn how to save lives with first aid, CPR, lifeguarding, HIV/AIDS education, and babysitter training are main parts of their work. They make great efforts to respond to the concerns of

Buehler A
Challenger
Space & Science Center 2006

people and kids at any location on Earth and at any time. This is an important organization, and the money from the space program would help the Red Cross and people around the world even more.

The ASPCA (American Society for the Prevention of Cruelty to Animals) is an organization that fights for the rights of animals. Animals help people with important jobs and can even be loving pets. The ASPCA tries to educate people about animals and increase awareness of animal cruelty. It also offers shelter, placement, and medical services to needy animals. This group can find a perfect home for animals, provide important training on how to care for them in our homes and communities, and teach kindness and respect. Their concern helps animals as well as people.

Greenpeace is very important in today's world because it focuses on our environment. Its goal is to prevent changes in our climate due to pollution. Acid rain and global warming are major problems. Greenpeace also wants to protect forests, save oceans, abolish nuclear weapons, and eliminate toxic chemicals. Our oceans are in serious trouble because fish and plants are dying of pollution and toxic chemicals. Yet we are spending our resources on space exploration rather than protecting life on Earth. We know more about Mars than we know about our oceans. Greenpeace's job is to help protect what is needed and enjoyed on Earth.

The three programs I have told you about, along with many, many more, are trying to respond to our present and future needs on Earth. We should support these programs by reassigning the space budget. The world would flourish, and people of today and tomorrow should live happier lives.

Consider the Moon

"The greatness of space exploration is that we are learning what is around us, and we're studying for the future."

—AMANDA PUNG

I didn't know much about the moon until I started my research and looked up some facts. And those facts didn't just appear out of thin air—many were discovered through space exploration. Space exploration has taught us a lot about the great places outside our Earth. This is excellent, because wouldn't you be scared if you didn't know about all the different things around you? The greatness of space exploration is that we are learning what is around us, and we're studying for the future. Part of our space exploration study began with the moon.

The moon is the only place a human has ever set foot, besides Earth. The NASA astronauts who landed on the moon in 1969 were Neil Armstrong and Edwin Eugene Aldrin, also known as "Buzz." Before they went, they trained doing static training, which simulated space-like conditions, and dynamic training, which prepared them for physical stresses of space flight. Even though it

Earth and its moon

doesn't sound like much now, their mission to the moon was a new beginning for space exploration in 1969.

Checking and recording oxygen levels in case of emergency

But what if the moon didn't exist? A great question with a great answer! If it didn't exist, Earth would rotate a lot faster, and our days would be shorter. That's because moon's gravity pulling on the oceans causes the ocean tides to ebb and flow, which slows down Earth's rotating. If Earth spun faster, winds could be amazingly fierce, which might make it hard for some species to exist. Aren't you glad the moon is around? Without it, we could be toast!

The moon is a satellite of Earth. It doesn't have any air or wind, but it does have ice, which is a sign of water. The ice was found by the space probe Clementine in 1996, and confirmed by the Lunar Prospector, a NASA Discovery mission, in January 1998. The thought of ice is good because then you think of water, and humans need that to survive. The bad part is that the ice is buried in freezing cold temperatures so that it is hard to unfreeze. An idea to unfreeze it is to use microwave energy. Scientists say that if we unfroze just one percent of the ice, there would be enough water for about 2,000 people for 500 years, and more if we recycled it! We could reuse it in different ways. It doesn't have to be just for drinking, but could also be for oxygen and fuel. Maybe there could be a space station on the moon! Would we know about that ice without space exploration? I think not.

Space exploration showed us that the moon is very different from Earth. At night the moon's surface becomes colder than any place on Earth. In the daytime, it becomes hotter than boiling! That means that people who go to the moon have to wear special clothes, not the everyday clothes we wear today. Another difference is that a day on the moon is about four weeks on Earth. Events wouldn't happen as quickly as they do on Earth, which is bad if you're waiting for an upcoming birthday, but good if you're going to the dentist. If we ever live on the moon, we would have to adapt to these changes. It will give us a great opportunity to learn more about using our resources to build a great plan if one is needed. I used my resources (facts found from space exploration) to build a great plan: this article!

We all have different feelings about space exploration. I believe that we should explore space because we can learn so many new things. And if something ever happens to our planet, we could move to a different one or find new resources, like the ice on the moon. So have I convinced you that space exploration is the way to go? Think about it!

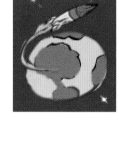

Buehler
Challenger
Space & Science Center 2006

Pro? Con? I Changed My Opinion

"All of the scientific advances that have come from our space program have contributed to the United States' good reputation worldwide." —ABIGAIL AGPAOA

I used to believe that we should not spend money on space exploration, but that we should spend it on Earth's needs. I believed that the money should be used to help people. But I've changed my mind. As I did my research for this book, I discovered that the money budgeted for space would probably not stop poverty on Earth. In fact, although many people believe what I used to believe, it appears that poverty is as much about the social issues in people's lives as it is about money. So, although it sounds strange, money may not necessarily be the cure for poverty.

The space exploration budget doesn't seem so expensive if you compare it to what some people spend on a daily basis. In 2004 Americans spent twice as much on pet-related merchandise than what we had budgeted for space exploration. Almost one

trillion dollars is spent each year on pets, toys, gambling, alcohol, and tobacco. That is 63 times the space exploration budget for 2005! Some people thought that the money Congress saved by stopping the funding of the Apollo missions to the moon might help rid us of poverty. That did not happen. The money was not necessarily given to the poor. Most people with extra money do not give it to the poor; instead, they go shopping.

I also found out that the money we do spend for space exploration actually does help our needs on Earth. It is not wasted. It allows new technologies to be developed. An example is that hospitals now have scanners (MRI and CAT) to help diagnose some illnesses. These came about when NASA was developing a way to take pictures of the moon. The advancement of technology also gets more young people interested in science and engineering, and in improving in our understanding of Earth and the entire universe.

Another fact that makes me believe that we should explore space is that NASA is a big contributor to the Climate Change Science Program, which provides information about changes to the environment that are caused by humans. The program helps scientists understand weather predictions, improve forecasts, track forest fires, and even learn how pollution is spread. The study of the sun contributes to this program. Technology advancements and the work of programs like the Climate Change Science Program also help people on Earth by providing more jobs. This is another plus in our explorations.

All of the scientific advances that have come from our space program have contributed to the United States' good reputation worldwide. That good reputation builds relationships with other countries, not only on space exploration, but also to improve life on Earth. And, at the same time, we get smarter and smarter.

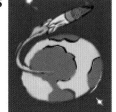

Should There Be Space Exploration?

Cast Your Vote

You've heard our arguments in favor of space exploration.

You've heard our arguments against space exploration.

It's time to cast your vote!

Authors at Work

How We Wrote Our Book

One day, Mrs. Harvey, our enrichment teacher, surprised us. She came to all the fifth grade classrooms and asked if there were any kids who liked to do research, who liked to write, and who might want to join a special project group. The tricky part was that she wouldn't tell us what the secret project might be. Eleven of us were brave enough to join the secret project group, and now here we are—the authors of this book.

1. We began our work by talking about topics we would like to research. After a number of suggestions, we decided to study space exploration. It seemed really cool and lots of fun. We didn't know that it was REALLY a hard one! Each day there seemed to be new and different information about space in the newspapers and on TV.

2. We made a "Should There Be Space Exploration?" survey (see p. 38) to help gather information from parents and other kids in our school. We spent a long time researching in the library, on the Internet, and in the books Mrs. Harvey had in her room. We had pages and pages of facts and our own thoughts about space.

3. Sometimes our research got all mixed up, and we were not sure what to do next. We brainstormed and put all our ideas and facts into categories on yellow stars that we hung on the wall. Separating our research into categories helped us know what each one of us believed.

4. Once again—research! Our job was to persuade others to agree with our thoughts, so it was important that we made sure that our research backed up our arguments.

5. When we started to write, we learned that persuasive writing needed:

   - a clearly stated opening that would grab the reader's attention

   - descriptive facts and opinions to support that opening

   - a strong ending that would pull all our facts and opinions together to convince others to agree with our thoughts

6. To make sure we were persuasive, we checked our work with each other to see if we were making our points. Then we started the second major part of writing this book—editing.

7. We edited our work somewhere between 4 and 8 times (someone in our group said it was about 100 times). It was pretty hard, but when it was time to type the final copy, it was a great feeling. We were all proud of each other and especially of ourselves.

8. After all the hard work, we spent some fun time making Moebius strips. They reminded us of what we already had learned through our research—that space never ends. Directions for making one are on p. 40.

Being an author was a lot more work than any one of us imagined. But even though we just told you about all the hard work involved in writing this book, nothing in school was more fun. We were able to work with each other, laugh over lunch in Mrs. Harvey's room, learn about things that others kids in our classes didn't know, and help each other on all parts of our work. One person in our group said something that we all agree with—we all felt special because we were representing our school.

So we hope you enjoyed our book. Someday we'd like to read yours!

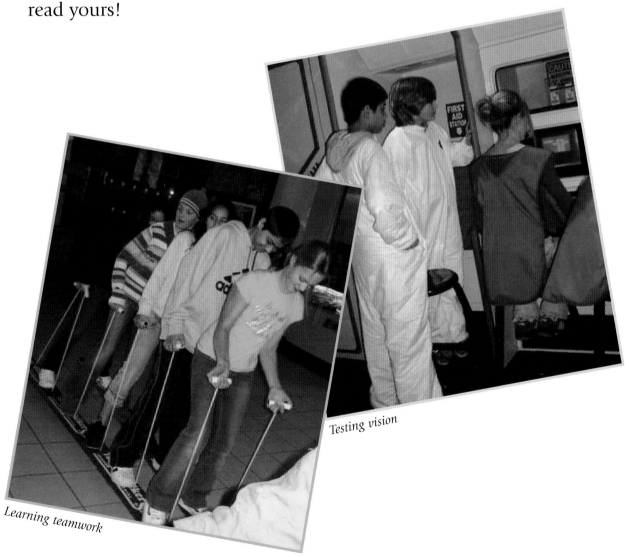

Testing vision

Learning teamwork

Should There Be Space Exploration?

Who? What? When? Where? Why? How? Should we? Those questions are necessary to meet the challenge that has been presented to 11 fifth graders by Mondo Publishing. The 11 authors have been given the task of writing a persuasive text about whether or not there should be space exploration in today's world. The students are looking at facts and opinions from children and adults. Your response to their survey will certainly be helpful and appreciated. Please return the survey with your child, or by mail, to the fifth grade authors at the school address. Feel free to make additional copies for others to complete. We will keep you informed about the 2006 publishing date.

1.	Do you often speak, read, or think about present-day space exploration?	YES	NO
2.	Do you think there is another planet like Earth?	YES	NO
3.	Do you want to learn about other planets?	YES	NO
4.	Do you believe there are useful things to discover (plants, medicines, etc.) on one of those planets?	YES	NO
5.	Do you believe there are aliens or extraterrestrials in outer space?	YES	NO
6.	Are there resources in space or on other planets that would be useful to us today?	YES	NO
7.	Should we allow people to risk their lives by exploring and experimenting with the unknown in space?	YES	NO
8.	Should we risk animals' lives by experimenting on them in space?	YES	NO
9.	Should we program robots to do explorations and experiments?	YES	NO
10.	Do you think there are places and resources on Earth that we should explore?	YES	NO
11.	Do you think the United States has enough money for space exploration and space projects?	YES	NO

12. Do you think the United States has enough money for Earth exploration and Earth projects?   YES   NO

13. Do you know what the International Space Station is?   YES   NO

14. Would you be willing to live in outer space to explore the future?   YES   NO

15. Would you be willing to live in another part of Earth to explore the future?   YES   NO

16. On a scale of 1 to 10 (1 being the lowest), how important do you think space exploration is in today's world?   1   2   3   4   5   6   7   8   9   10

17. On a scale of 1 to 10 (1 being the lowest), how important do you think Earth exploration is in today's world?   1   2   3   4   5   6   7   8   9   10

18. Please explain answers 16 and 17. Any thoughts or comments will help us form our opinions about whether we should explore space in our lifetime. Thank you.

_____

_____

_____

_____

_____

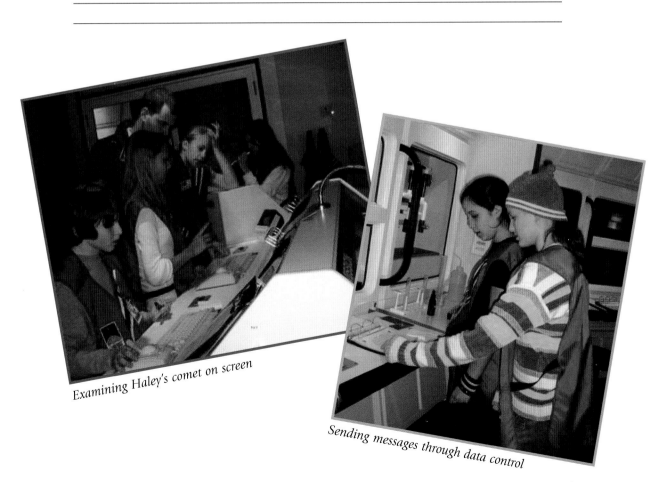

Examining Haley's comet on screen

Sending messages through data control

Moebius Strip

Trying to understand the universe is a bit overwhelming. Does it ever end? Does it go on forever and ever? We don't know, and even the world's most brilliant people have questions about it.

We made a Moebius strip out of a piece of paper to help us see how something might not have an end. The Moebius strip is named after a 19th century German mathematician, A.F. Möbius. We'd like to share how we made it. Maybe it will help you understand the never-ending universe.

1. Cut a strip of paper that is about 16 inches (40 cm) long and 1 inch (2.5 cm) wide.

2. Hold one end of the strip in each hand. Twist one end halfway around. Put another way, give one end a half turn.

3. Glue the ends together, keeping the half twist. It will look a bit like a crooked oval.

When you run your finger around the strip, you will see that there is no beginning and no end. What do you think might happen if you cut the strip right down the middle? Try it!

Sizing the moon proportionately to Earth

(Earth is 49 times larger than the moon.)

Glossary

alien	a creature from outer space; an extraterrestrial being
American Red Cross	an organization that helps with disasters and major emergencies
Apollo	a program of space missions between 1967–1975 that put 12 men on the moon.
ASPCA	an organization that fights for the rights of animals
astronaut	a person who is trained to travel and work in space
astronomer	a scientist who studies things outside Earth's atmosphere
atmosphere	gases that surround planets and other space bodies
bus	holds all instruments in payload and keeps satellite going
CAT	computed axial tomography, or the use of computers to create three-dimensional images from x-rays
Clementine	lunar orbiter launched in 1994 that found evidence of ice on the moon
con	against something
CPR	cardiopulmonary resuscitation; an emergency procedure to help restart breathing and circulation until help comes
Dog Laika	the first dog sent into space, aboard Russia's Sputnik II in 1957
drag	a force that slows down a body moving through air because the body is moving in an opposite direction from the air
dust storm	dust lifted into air by lack of gravity

Gordo	a space-traveling squirrel monkey that died in 1958
GPS	Global Positioning System; a navigation instrument
Greenpeace	international organization for environmental conservation and endangered species protection
Hubble Space Telescope	an orbiting space telescope
ISS	International Space Station
James Webb Telescope	possible Hubble replacement
Jupiter AM-13 rocket	booster rocket that Gordo rode and died in
lag time	with robots, the time between the command and the reaction
light second	the distance that light travels in one second
Lunar Prospector	NASA discovery mission launched in 1998 that found evidence of ice on the moon
Martian	an alien, or extraterrestrial, from Mars
meteorologist	scientist who studies the atmosphere, weather, and weather forecasting
microbes	a microscopic bit of live matter that can develop into a living organism
microgravity	a state of weightlessness
MRI	magnetic resonance imaging, or a technique that can produce very detailed computer-generated images of the inside of the body
NASA	National Aeronautics and Space Administration
nebula	the death of a star
orbit	an invisible path that circles the globe or another body
payload	cameras and other equipment needed on satellites to do the work
pro	in favor of something
robot	a machine or device guided by remote or automatic controls

satellites	natural or man-made objects or vehicles that orbit bodies in space
sensor	a device that receives and responds to signals
simulated mission	a training procedure that creates space-travel conditions on Earth similar to those in space
Skylab	a science and engineering lab launched into Earth orbit by a Saturn rocket in 1973 and manned by Apollo astronauts
solar cells	cells that convert sunlight into electricity
solar energy	energy from the sun
solar panels	connected solar cells
space shuttle	the first reusable spacecraft. It carries large satellites into orbit. It is launched like a rocket, it flies around Earth like a spaceship, and it lands like an airplane. NASA plans to retire the space shuttle by 2010.
Sputnik	the first man-made satellite, launched by the Soviet Union in 1957
squirrel monkey	a long-tailed monkey from Central and South America
toxic	poisonous

Communicating with Mission Control

Index

Assembling probe to gather Haley's comet sample

More team-building!

Communicating with Mission Control and examining Haley's comet

ANSWER:

A superstar!